To Eric,
With Love and Best Wishes!
Dec. 17, 1989
Mom & John

WHICH NICHE?

by Jack Shingleton
illustrations by Phil Frank

BOB ADAMS, INC.
PUBLISHERS

ISBN: 1-55850-999-2

Published by Bob Adams, Inc., 260 Center Street,
Holbrook MA 02343.

Printed in the United States of America.

CONTENTS

a cover letter when you send your resume to an employer? (63)/ How long should your resume be? (65)/ Is military, summer, co-op, or part-time employment important? (67)/ Should you apply to a private employment agency? (69)/ What about drug tests? (71)/ Is salary the only "carrot" you'll be offered? (73)/ Is your grade point average important in landing a job? (75)/ How much importance do employers place on school activities? (77)

Chapter Three: The All-Important Interview/79

What should you do before the interview? (81)/ What questions are asked in the interview? (83)/ What kind of interviews can you expect? (85)/ How do you answer interview questions? (87)/ What shouldn't you bring up at the interview? (89)/ When interviewing--do: (91)/ When interviewing--don't: (93)/ Will my spouse be "interviewed"? (95)/ What is the "stress interview"? (97)/ How do you handle "off the wall" interview questions? (99)/ Who pays travel expenses for out-of-town interviews? (101)/ How do you handle the group interview? (103)/ What salary should you ask for? (105)/ When should you discuss fringe benefits? (107)

Chapter Four: Making Your Decision/109

Is your first job your lifetime job? (111)/ Avoid pointless job changes (113)/ What if you get an offer, accept it, and then receive a better offer? (115)/ Will you have to take tests? (117)/ When the job seeks you out . . . (119)/ Which is better: joining a company with a formal training program, or one without such a program? (121)/ What is the usual procedure when an offer is made? (123)/ What is the usual procedure when accepting a job? (125)

Chapter Five: Evaluating Your Progress/127

You must be new here.

INTRODUCTION

A week or so after the average person reports to work for the first time, doubts set in. "Did I pick the right field?" "Did I choose the right type of company?" "Somehow the world of professional employment isn't all I dreamed it would be. Why?"

This book is intended to prepare you to go about entering the best possible career for you--and help you minimize second-guessing--by making the right choices the first time through. The twofold faced by many job seekers (choosing a career and getting the right jobs during your career) carries immense implications--not only from a financial standpoint, but also when it comes to personal fulfillment. What follows is designed to help you make the most of that task for your own sake . . . and your employer's!

WHICH NICHE? is a collection of answers to the most frequently asked career questions from recent high school and college graduates; others seeking jobs early in a career will find the advice contained within these covers useful as well.

WHICH NICHE? was the theme selected by the students of Michigan State University for the school's annual career program. The program was so popular with students and alumni that many suggested it form the basis of a book. A privately circulated edition met with great success, and eventually became the present version, revised and expanded to meet the needs of those trying to make sense of today's job market.

WHICH NICHE?--the title--still sums up precisely the quandary in which many job seekers find themselves. And *WHICH NICHE?*--the book--offers the answers in a concise, easy-to-understand style.

Good luck!

Jack Shingleton

CHAPTER ONE: CHOOSING THE RIGHT CAREER

Our son, an attorney....
Where did we fail him?

WHAT IS YOUR MAIN OBJECTIVE IN SELECTING A CAREER?

The main objective is to make the choices that will provide you with a life of satisfaction, challenge, and personal fulfillment. That may or may not include making a great deal of money. Each person must define these crucial goals individually, and while making the right choices is not easy, it *can* be done with proper planning.

Remember, a college degree is not a guarantee of success. Economic returns are usually not the final measure of success. The main objective in seeking the right career niche for you is to find that career that suits you intellectually, socially, psychologically, and economically.

According to your resumé you're trustworthy, loyal, helpful, friendly, courteous, kind, cheerful, thrifty, and brave.

WHAT DO YOU HAVE TO OFFER?

Most people don't realize their full potential--and undersell themselves. They don't think enough about their talents and abilities and are reluctant to exploit the genuine advantages they present to an employer.

Sit down and list your abilities, talents, and shortcomings. This is the most objective way to find out what you have to offer. If you have a reliable friend, relative or teacher who will assist you in compiling such a list, ask for their help.

Remember that in terms of both employer perception and personal ability, your education is one of your most important assets. If you are trying to decide whether or not to complete the work necessary to attain your diploma or college degree, the answer is almost always "do so." Al Smith, the legendary governor of New York, put it very well when he said, "If you doubt the value of an education, ask the man who never had one."

Initially, the best objective is to know yourself. Once you understand the "package" you present, and match it with the proper area of endeavor, you will be well on your way toward a successful and rewarding career.

They don't pay much where
I work, but... Boy— the prestige!

WHAT ARE YOU LOOKING FOR IN A CAREER?

Money? Authority? Prestige? Security? Social advancement? Personal growth? All of the above?

Half the battle of winning the right job is knowing what you want out of a career--and out of life. Define what you want and then go after it.

Be sure that you are fitted for the employment area you select, and that you have a natural interest in it. You will not be a success on your own terms if you win a high-salaried job doing something you loathe. (For that matter, you will probably not be a success on anyone's terms.)

Career goals change as you go through life. It is important, however, that you have a sense of direction. Try to establish your most important goals early on (perhaps even as you go through high school and/or college, if you're still in school). Get a good, basic idea of what you are looking for in your career and plan accordingly.

The world of work is probably where you'll make your greatest contribution--to yourself and to the rest of the world. In our society, work is what we spend most of our time doing, and is our primary means of self-expression. Recognize the importance your job will hold in relating to your world.

Do you have any reasons for wanting to work in a brewery other than you like beer?

SHOULD YOU PLAN AHEAD OR IMPROVISE?

The most important part of getting the right job is to plan ahead. Very often the difference between happiness and misery is your job, and making it up as you go along can have disastrous consequences when it comes to career development. Life is too short to be spent doing work you don't enjoy.

Henry David Thoreau said that most people "live lives of quiet desperation." Nowhere is that more true than in the world of work. Too often our focus in thinking about our work is on salary, benefits, and title. The real winners, however, are those who truly enjoy their work and find satisfaction and fulfillment in what they do. So be prepared to do a little homework in order to find the right job for you.

During the Depression there were far more people seeking work than there were jobs. Almost every high school or college graduate who wants to work, however, can get a job today. Take advantage of this opportunity. Take the time to learn what opportunities await you. Avoid snap decisions.

I had **no** idea there was such a shortage of engineers..

WHY DO PEOPLE CHANGE JOBS?

The reasons include:

Personality conflicts with associates.
Dissatisfaction with overall situation.
Desire for more money.
Personal reasons (including feelings of stagnation).
Desire for more recognition.
Lack of proper qualifications in current job.
Better chance for advancement elsewhere.
Desire for a change of locations.

It's easier to change jobs today because:

Society is more mobile.
Job information resources are plentiful and of high quality.
Competition among employers for competent personnel is keen.
Job mobility is more acceptable.
There are many opportunities available for those who will take the time and effort to find them.

I think you're combining home and office a bit too much...

"LIVE TO WORK, WORK TO LIVE"?

The job is one segment of the pie--but not the whole pie. The other segments include family life, overall day-to-day fulfillment, community activities, living environment, leisure time, long-term personal goals, and various other factors, depending upon the individual.

While all of these factors are important, for most of us the reality is that work is our primary activity. On average, a person will spend approximately 100,000 hours of his or her life working. Make those hours worthwhile and rewarding--but don't forget about the other aspects of life!

Most people do not spend enough time evaluating their job as it relates to their whole life--and then wonder why happiness eludes them. Make a commitment to yourself to examine your full potential and then carry out a job search strategy that's consistent with your goals.

In addition, you might ask yourself: how many people, lying on their deathbeds, choose "I wish I had spent more time with the business" as last words?

WHAT SHOULD YOU LOOK FOR IN A JOB?

Only you can answer this. The "right" answer will be based on your likes, dislikes, talents, and willingness to work. Ultimately, you must define what you want and then compare that with what you can contribute. The two categories should be roughly equivalent. If they aren't, either you or the employer are getting shortchanged. This situation usually results in an unproductive relationship for one or (more likely) both parties.

A list of items to consider:

> What do you enjoy doing?
>
> What are you good at doing?
>
> How important is money to you?
>
> Do you want to travel?
>
> Do you want a high-risk or a low-risk job?
>
> How hard do you want to work?
>
> Is prestige important to you?
>
> What do you have to offer?
>
> Do you have the educational background necessary for the job?
>
> If you perform well, where will you end up?
>
> Will there continue to be a demand for the type of work you choose?
>
> Are you well suited for the job?
>
> Do you have a great interest in the work?
>
> When retirement comes, will you be able to look back on a satisfying career?

IF YOU'RE IN SCHOOL, SHOULD YOU STAY THERE--OR TAKE TIME OFF TO "FIND OUT WHAT YOU WANT TO DO"?

Stay in school.

Don't be a dropout! Though there are a very few dropouts who are millionaires, the odds are stacked heavily against such luck. If you want to "find yourself," do so while you're still in high school or college--and adjust your curriculum accordingly.

Career exploration belongs on every student's agenda. It's not a one-shot deal to be considered the month before you graduate, or over a "year off" (which many extend indefinitely). Career exploration is something that goes on (or should go on) beginning in high school, continuing through college, and afterwards. When it comes to strategies and career exploration, however, students are at a distinct advantage compared to those already in the workforce . . . because students have many more options open to them and much more flexibility!

It's not easy to set career and personal goals, much less develop strategies, while you're still in the "exploratory" mode associated with high school or college. But with the proper effort, motivation, persistence and determination, your "groundwork" can have a tremendous positive impact on your later life.

Aha! Decided to finalize
your plans, I see...

HOW IMPORTANT IS A COLLEGE EDUCATION?

A diploma, of course, is a big advantage in most job searches. How much of an advantage is up to the individual.

The better the job you do in planning your formal education, the better your chances of success in career planning and in the job market. Of course, students who know that they eventually want to go into specialized fields such as accounting, medicine, law, engineering, mathematics, or education have an easier time focusing on the subjects they must study in school. Liberal arts students often have difficulty choosing a specific career area. However, a four year degree in the liberal arts can form the basis of a strong "candidate package"--especially when coupled with an advanced degree in a specialty.

If you have difficulty in defining your career goals, a liberal arts curriculum will give you a broader base than many other curricula. You'll have the advantage of a broader perspective than some other disciplines before finally committing yourself to a chosen field. The one pitfall here is that liberal arts majors sometimes procrastinate too long before making career plans. Sometimes they end up with a degree and no plan whatsoever.

Several surveys have shown that successful business and industry executives come from all educational backgrounds, with no particular discipline predominating. In the final analysis, the individual makes the difference. Whatever you choose, solid academic performance coupled with worthwhile work experiences will add greatly to your potential.

I decided to earn my
two million all at once.

WHAT'S THE JOB POTENTIAL
FOR THE RECENT COLLEGE GRADUATE?

Excellent--especially if the graduate carries out a well-planned search for a job. In addition to the opportunities discussed earlier for those with sound liberal arts credentials, there is strong demand for bachelor degree graduates in the technical, scientific, accounting, business and educational fields. Most graduates from accredited institutions should have a job before graduation or shortly thereafter. Natural resources and agricultural graduates with bachelors degrees have more competition, but those who are persistent always end up with a job.

Advanced degrees generally increase your starting salary and open many doors into highly specialized fields not open to persons with less education. Lifetime earnings of the average college graduate is estimated at over two million dollars.

Next to choosing your spouse, the most important decision you will make in your lifetime is probably choosing the career you are going to follow. When you have a multi-million-dollar decision to make (and that's what your job search amounts to), you had better make the most of it. Still, some people put more time, effort and energy into buying an automobile than they do planning a career.

Is a college education worth the time and expense? Yes. Most college graduates make substantially more in a lifetime than those with a high school education only. Those extra years of education pay off handsomely.

You don't have to take the
First job that comes along....

DO YOU HAVE TO CHOOSE A CAREER RELATED TO YOUR COLLEGE STUDY?

Not necessarily. Many people have successful careers in areas of employment completely unrelated to their academic studies.

That having been said, remember that in many cases you will put yourself at a competitive disadvantage by pursuing work unrelated to your background. You will have lost valuable time by changing direction, and you will need to learn the basics of the new field without the benefit of courses you could have taken earlier.

Some students simply cannot make up their minds about what they want to do until several years after graduation. This is usually both costly and frustrating. However, should you find that the field of work for which you have studied is not what you enjoy doing, don't be afraid to change. The sooner you do so, the better.

I used to work in Personnel but now there aren't any personnel...

DO MOST PEOPLE WORK IN THEIR AREA OF COLLEGE TRAINING?

Most do when they start their careers. As they gain new experiences, they sort out their likes and dislikes, find new opportunities and interests, and spin off into all kinds of career paths they hadn't thought of earlier.

Most people do not end up in the specific field for which they studied. The more specialized the college training, however, the more likely it is that the person will remain in the field of specialization. This is particularly true of certain professions (for instance, medicine and law).

ARE EMPLOYERS INTERESTED IN CANDIDATES WITH A MILITARY COMMITMENT?

The attitudes of employers with regard to this question can vary. Chief concerns include the state of the labor market and the specific military commitment the candidate has. The more an employer wants you, the more he or she is likely to adjust to your military status.

College graduates with an R.O.T.C. or similar commitment usually wait until they are in the final six to twelve months of fulfilling their military obligation before interviewing for a job.

Military service can be a useful alternative for people just finishing high school or college without firm ideas about the types of careers attractive to them. Other advantages of military service include the development of managerial skills, exposure to the latest technology, improvement of written and verbal skills, and on-the-job training and continuing education.

I just went in to use the phone and I got a $29,000 a year job. I start Tuesday.

WHERE SHOULD YOU GO TO
LOOK FOR CAREER OPPORTUNITIES?

In most cases, there are more opportunities than anywhere else at your college placement office (which is, typically, open to alumni as well as students). It's probably the best place to get objective information on your career planning.

This is not to say that you should rely entirely on the placement office as the focus of your entire job search campaign; your personal contacts and other outreach efforts should complement the work you do at the placement office. Nevertheless, it's an excellent idea to get to know your placement officer; he or she can be a vital source of career information.

CHAPTER TWO: REACHING YOUR OBJECTIVES

Have you decided what part of the country you'd prefer working in?

WHAT ISSUES SHOULD BE RESOLVED BEFORE BEGINNING THE JOB SEARCH?

Many graduates interview for jobs without having firmed up their thinking regarding basic objectives. These objectives must incorporate such factors as military service, geographic preference, graduate school, whether one prefers to work for a large or a small company, and numerous other matters that should usually be addressed before the job search begins in earnest.

Resolve such items properly before interviewing. You will reduce the complexities of an already challenging situation and save yourself a lot of time, money and energy.

WHAT ABOUT GOAL-SETTING?

Most people do not set their goals high enough and never realize their full potential. Good career planning begins with knowing and believing in yourself.

Setting high goals, however, must be accompanied by energy, effort, intelligence and interest. It is helpful to remind yourself periodically of your goals.

DON'T CHANGE JOBS FOR THE WRONG REASONS

The notion that changing jobs will, by definition, lead to better working conditions is, unfortunately, a common one. Many job changes result in significantly worse employment situations. Changing jobs impulsively, without thinking through all the factors involved in the switch, almost always results in greater career dissatisfaction.

Too often, people change jobs for the wrong reasons: fleeting personality conflicts, a bad day at the office, or ill-timed criticism from the boss. These are not good reasons to make major career changes.

Here are some questions you might ask yourself when considering a change:

> Is the "culture" of the new employer in consonance with my values?
>
> What will be the impact on my family?
>
> What costs related to housing, moving and getting re-established will I incur?
>
> What are my long-run expectations in the new job compared to my current job?
>
> Specifically, why am I changing jobs? Will that reason be forgotten in a few days or weeks? If so, why change?

WHAT ARE THE ADVANTAGES OF GOING INTO BUSINESS FOR YOURSELF?

You'll have the satisfaction of being your own boss and, if successful, achieve a large measure of security. You will not have to report to anyone. On the other hand, many people are not as productive when they supervise themselves as when they work for someone else. There is also the real possibility that your enterprise can fail.

It usually takes capital to start a business, as well as the ability to handle high-risk situations. The personal satisfaction you derive from running your own business can be high, but so can the disappointment.

You must have great desire and stamina to overcome adversities. You must be a self starter. If you possess these qualities, and are willing to work very hard for a long period of time, you may well succeed in your own business--providing your product or service fills a customer need. Before deciding to begin a business, you are strongly urged to consult a counselor, qualified retired executive, or successful colleague.

In this profession it takes more education. I graduated three weeks ago Friday...

WHAT ARE THE ADVANTAGES OF ENTERING A PROFESSION?

The road to success in professions such as law or medicine is long and hard. Achieving career goals here involves a great deal of work, tenacity, and sacrifice. Do not choose a profession unless you are personally secure in the choice, dedicated to success, and committed to the principles of the discipline.

The financial rewards can be great. So can elements such as prestige, the ability to help others, and job satisfaction. A profession requires years of preparation, however, as well as the capacity to meet rigorous academic standards. Income is delayed for several years compared to most other fields of work, a factor that can lead to considerable demands upon one's family and/or spouse.

We're a small firm...but
we're very close.

WHAT ARE THE ADVANTAGES OF
WORKING FOR A SMALL COMPANY?

You'll have the opportunity to learn about many aspects of the business in a comparatively short period of time. You'll be closer to top management. Your successes will be more likely to be visible ones.

However, chances of advancement are often limited (due to the scarcity of management positions), and family politics can be a problem. Risks are greater than in the large corporation since the small company is more likely to go out of business. However, over time the rewards may be greater. In the beginning, your work schedule is likely to feature long hours.

The work environment in a small company is usually less structured than that of larger firms. Responsibilities tend to be more diversified, with less of a bureaucratic feel to the proceedings.

Small companies do not have the support systems large companies have, but your abilities and accomplishments are more measurable in the smaller firm's work environment.

We're looking for someone
who's willing to start at the
bottom... and stay there.

WHAT ARE THE ADVANTAGES OF WORKING FOR A LARGE COMPANY?

Good training and a lot of help in the early years are probably the biggest pluses. Job security is often better than if you worked for a small firm. Your progress will depend to some degree upon seniority; this carries with it the possibility of getting lost in the crowd. Pay tends to be good and growth continuous (if not always dramatic) if you are a steady producer.

In addition, job mobility is increased in the large organizations due to the greater number of positions available. And fringe benefits in large organizations are, as a rule, better than those in small companies.

A significant disadvantage: you are subject to the whims and predispositions of decision-makers to whom you are likely to have no access. Many people do not work well within a hierarchical structure; for such employees a job in a large firm will present serious challenges.

I have just the job in mind for someone who's interested in cleaning up the country.

WHAT ARE THE ADVANTAGES OF GOVERNMENT EMPLOYMENT?

Government work can provide a solid career path, as long as you have a certain amount of patience and don't aspire to an executive-level salary. There are opportunities in all fields and the pay is acceptable, though unlikely to make anyone a millionaire.

Government employment places heavy emphasis on seniority and security. If your goal is to "get on the fast track," you will be frustrated at times. The government hiring process usually takes a little longer. Starting pay varies depending upon geographic location. Fringe benefits are very good.

There are numerous opportunities in the public sector. Keep in mind that there are various levels of government employment: municipal, county, state and federal. Within each you will find an abundance of agencies, departments, commissions, and other bodies--all of which have turnover just like companies do. Explore opportunities in all these areas, and you may find the position that's right for you.

WHAT ARE THE OPPORTUNITIES
FOR WORKING ABROAD?

Opportunities for working abroad are increasing all the time. Jobs for graduates fresh out of college are scarce, though. The best way to get a job abroad is to join an international organization, establish yourself, and make known your interest in working abroad. This will take time, but there is little chance of changing the way these decisions are made. Employers usually send their most competent people abroad because of the costs involved, and prefer not to make the investment in an unproven employee.

The Peace Corps offers short-term opportunities overseas, but these assignments are not usually career-oriented. The work environment in the Peace Corps is entirely different from that of corporations, though such work does serve as an impressive resume-builder. United States Agency for International Development (U.S.A.I.D.) is also a good source of overseas jobs, as is the State Department. In addition, those interested in education can find many teaching opportunities at military installations abroad.

International employment is not for everyone. There are many cultural and social stresses, and if these are coupled with job dissatisfaction, the situation can become quite unpleasant. Be sure you evaluate any foreign job offer very carefully before accepting the assignment.

I think you could drop those two paragraphs about your ant farm...

WHAT IS A RESUME?

A resume is an advertisement you write about yourself to help convince the employer how much you have to offer his or her company. Specifically, a resume is a short biography that tells an employer what you have done. Typically, the resume includes:

> Contact information: address and telephone number where you may be reached.
>
> Employment goals: type of employment sought, areas of employment interest, goals sought.
>
> Education: institutions attended, degrees received and when, grade point, degree of self-support (optional).
>
> Experience/Accomplishments: applicable part-time, summer, military employment. (List all full-time employment, highlighting tangible successes in past positions wherever possible.)
>
> Activities: student organizations, professional societies, civic activities.
>
> References: professional and character names and addresses (optional).

In some instances it may also be appropriate to include some personal information, such as hobbies or outside interests, if these reinforce the message you are trying to convey and highlight skills. Putting down your life experiences in chronological form can help you understand-- before the job hunt--the sequence of events that led to your current status. Remember that the final version must make sense from the employer's perspective. (Note: If you are applying for many jobs, one resume may not fill all your needs.)

Saaay... you must be quite the guy...

WHAT IS THE PURPOSE OF A RESUME?

A resume serves many purposes.

It can initiate or reinforce an employer's decision to interview you.

It helps you determine and define your assets, liabilities, and objectives before you interview.

It supplements your regular application.

It can open doors beyond the reach of your personal contacts network.

It can project your strongest qualifications in a positive, professional manner.

It can be helpful when filling out employers' application forms.

It can be part of your permanent employee record and provide information your employer might not receive in the regular application form.

SHOULD YOU INCLUDE A COVER LETTER WHEN YOU SEND YOUR RESUME TO AN EMPLOYER?

By all means. The letter is as important as the resume and should be written with a great deal of thought and, like the resume, focused on the employer's needs. This is where you can personalize your correspondence by focusing your talents to the problems faced by the particular employer to whom you are writing. Your resume may be too general in content to do this.

A good cover letter can also suggest to the employer any specific skills and pertinent information not included in the resume. Close your letter of application with an "action" ending. Request a personal interview with the employer as soon as possible, or suggest a date when you will try to contact the employer.

Don't use your current employer's stationery. This suggests you are using your employer's time to apply for other employment.

Judging from your resume
you haven't really done a lot...

HOW LONG SHOULD YOUR RESUME BE?

One page is usually adequate. Two or more pages may be acceptable depending upon your education and experience. Generally, the best resumes are brief, hard-hitting, and slanted toward the employer's needs. References may be included, but are not essential.

That's a nicely peeled potato— but did the military teach you anything about electronics?

IS MILITARY, SUMMER, CO-OP
OR PART-TIME EMPLOYMENT IMPORTANT?

Yes! It's especially important if it is related to your career plans. Career-related work will also help with your studies since it helps you incorporate real-life insights to supplement your theoretical knowledge.

Career-related military, summer, co-op or part time employment can help boost your starting salary offer when you do win your first full-time job. Many employers recruit students for summer and co-op opportunities with the hope of hiring them permanently upon graduation.

SHOULD YOU APPLY TO A
PRIVATE EMPLOYMENT AGENCY?

If you've just graduated, your college placement office is often a better route. It's frequently more helpful than a service in helping alumni find the right jobs, too.

Employment agencies are businesses, operated for profit. They charge a fee, either to the employee or employer, depending upon the arrangements made. If you're paying, there's a good chance you could do the same job yourself for nothing. If the employer is paying, you will probably find that the competition is just as fierce as it would be if you weren't using the service.

On the other hand, candidates for executive positions (such as recent recipients of advanced degrees, or persons with significant work experience), frequently find the private agency a workable method for getting a new job. If you fall into this category, and wish to work with an agency, proceed with caution. While there are many good firms specializing in this field (almost always employer-fee-paid), there are a few unscrupulous outfits that will charge exorbitant fees to circulate your resume to employers randomly, with little chance of results that justify what you pay.

Perhaps you misunderstood.. L.S.D. stands for Libbey, Spears, Durham.

WHAT ABOUT DRUG TESTS?

More and more companies are screening applicants for illicit drug use. Pre-employment drug screening typically takes two forms: direct questioning and laboratory testing. Initial inquiries about drug use may appear on a questionnaire or employment application. Many employers screen for drugs during pre-employment (and sometimes post-employment) health examinations. If applicants refuse to submit to drug testing, their candidacy is usually terminated.

Already, these practices have resulted in some disputes between employers and prospective employees. While not all companies screen for drug use, the trend is toward more, not less, testing, and applicants should be prepared to respond to inquiries in this area--or target job search efforts elsewhere if they object on philosophical or other grounds to such tests.

Oh.. and one last thing ... we do not have any pay difference between men and women. **Everybody** gets paid the same paltry, piddling amount..

IS SALARY THE ONLY
"CARROT" YOU'LL BE OFFERED?

In the past, employer motivational systems were based upon the offer of economic rewards--and the possible threat of punishment or termination--to boost employee performance.

In recent years the system has been changing. The college graduate, now in a better bargaining position than in times past, strives for more personal dignity, more ongoing education, more self expression, and more meaningful opportunities--not just a good salary.

Therefore, today's graduate seeks a job that is challenging in and of itself, as well as a work environment conducive to growth and self-fulfillment. Wise employers are striving to offer these as part of a total employment "package," in order to reduce turnover and hold on to the very best people.

Pretty proud of that grade point average, eh, son?

IS YOUR GRADE POINT AVERAGE IMPORTANT IN LANDING A JOB?

It can be, especially for your initial job. If you have been in the work force for more than a year or so, the significance of your grade point average (GPA) lessens.

One of the main reasons the GPA is important to employers considering recent graduates is that it is one of the few elements that can be measured with some degree of accuracy and used as a "yardstick" from candidate to candidate. Most factors used in judging prospects are not so clear-cut. Remember, however, that while a good grade point point average may help in getting a job, it's not much help in keeping it. School is a very different environment than work. More emphasis is placed on personal initiative, goal orientation, and creativity in the office than in most classrooms. Also important to most employers: subjects taken, special achievements, personality, appearance, and general attitude toward work and the employing organization.

Homecoming Queen **and** band..
..quite impressive..

HOW MUCH IMPORTANCE DO EMPLOYERS PLACE ON SCHOOL ACTIVITIES?

It depends on your background, the company you want to work for, and the type of job you are seeking. For recent graduates, campus activities can be important in jobs that involve organizing and meeting people, but campus activities alone are usually not enough.

As with your GPA, school activities diminish in importance the longer you have been in the work force.

CHAPTER THREE: THE ALL-IMPORTANT INTERVIEW

I was just doing a little research on the company before my interview...

WHAT SHOULD YOU DO
BEFORE THE INTERVIEW?

Research!

Researching the prospective employer before your interview is a must. It not only helps you understand the company better, but also gives you a chance to display your knowledge of the company as a strong selling point!

Check your local library for sources of information on employers, special directories, lists of relevant associations, trade journals, and/or professional publications. Most high school and university placement offices have career information where these materials are also available. In addition, you should contact the public relations department of the company and ask for promotional materials to review.

WHAT QUESTIONS ARE ASKED IN THE INTERVIEW?

This depends entirely upon the interviewer and the kind of interview being conducted. Some of the more frequent questions asked include:

How would you describe yourself?
What are you looking for in a job?
Elaborate on your resume.
What do you consider your strengths or weaknesses?
Why did you select your major?
What do you consider your greatest accomplishment?
What do you expect in a salary?
What can you offer a company like ours?
Elaborate on your work (or: co-op) experience?
Why did you choose to interview with our company?
Are you prepared to travel (or: relocate)?
When are you available to start work?

These are but a few of the dozens you may be asked. Your answers should convey professionalism, accomplishment, honesty, diligence, and grace under pressure. Wherever and wherever appropriate, pass along stories that highlight your productivity, efficiency, and profit-orientation. Prepare winning answers for questions like those above--but expect the unexpected as well!

You may find our interviews
a little different...

WHAT KIND OF INTERVIEWS CAN YOU EXPECT?

The Screening Interview. Used to identify several candidates from a large number. Usually, the interview is short and may be conducted in person or by phone.

The Personal Interview. The candidate is interviewed in-depth by a representative of the company (though not necessarily by the person to whom he or she would report).

The Group Interview. Several representatives of the employer interview and screen the candidate. This is almost always preceded by a personal interview.

The Structured Interview. A candidate is presented with specific, predetermined questions, and follows a set routine that many other applicants repeat exactly.

The Unstructured Interview. The candidate is asked to give a brief history of experience and education relating to the job, followed by more detailed questions pertaining to his or her qualifications. This is sometimes coupled with a "situation interview" where the employer defines certain situations or problems, and then asks how the candidate would handle them.

The Stress Interview. Typically used when the position in question is a high-risk or stress-oriented job requiring quick analysis of facts and the ability to make good decisions under duress. The candidate may be openly challenged or presented with a barrage of confusing problems to solve.

HOW DO YOU ANSWER
INTERVIEW QUESTIONS?

It's not enough to supply only the information sufficient to address the interviewer's query. You must use your response time to highlight the assets you would bring to the company.

You have a limited time to "sell" your candidacy. Don't leave it to the recruiter to try to find out all your capabilities; he or she may not conduct a good interview. It is your responsibility to communicate all the benefits you would bring to the firm. Use concrete examples that increase effectiveness or profitability. "Toot your own horn," but do so in a way that conveys confident professionalism.

Remember, if the employer does not know all your strong points, you are essentially asking that he or she give the job to someone else. Many employers are not good interviewers. Follow the interviewer's lead, and do not challenge. Don't wait for the right questions--give the right answers.

How about one more verse of
"The Saints Come Marchin' In"...
..as you go marchin' out?

WHAT SHOULDN'T YOU
BRING UP AT THE INTERVIEW?

The interview is no place for idealistic discourses on politics, religion, or social justice. Introducing such topics is an excellent way to convince someone you should not be hired.

Companies are in business to make money; successful people within them tend to be more realistic than idealistic. Make an effort to understand the mindset of the organization where you hope to work. Don't go out of your way to challenge that mindset. You should not ask yourself to compromise a deeply-held conviction; you should, however, use discretion on controversial subjects. If the interviewer happens to bring up a political, social, or religious issue about which you have strong feelings, your best option is to respond politely and honestly, but to avoid open (and possibly inflammatory) pronouncements.

No need to be nervous about an interview, son...

WHEN INTERVIEWING--DO:

Be as calm and composed as possible.

Be neat and properly dressed.

Be prepared to answer common questions.

Be aware that you may encounter questions for which you have not prepared.

Research your employer.

Bring extra copies of your resume.

Know your graduate school plans.

Know your geographic requirements.

Know whether you would be willing to travel.

Know the salary range you expect. Try to be both optimistic and realistic in this regard.

Know your references and their contact information.

Ask questions about the job.

Finish the interview with a positive course of action ("May I call you on [date] to confirm my status?")

Keep a written record of all interviews. Negotiations, plant visits, oral commitments, and correspondence can get confusing.

My pen leaks..

WHEN INTERVIEWING--DON'T

Present an unprofessional image (by dressing inappropriately or filling out forms sloppily, to give two examples).

Take other people with you to the interview.

Use profanity.

Be overbearing or argumentative.

Be afraid to look the interviewer in the eye.

Condemn former employers, faculty or associates.

Be late.

Be discourteous to the administrative staff.

Behave differently outside the interview room than you would within it.

Bring up controversial subjects.

Does he eat all his vegetables?

WILL MY SPOUSE BE "INTERVIEWED"?

Sometimes. At the higher levels of employment, there is a greater chance that your spouse will be invited to some element of the selection process. Often this "interview" will be at a lunch or dinner meeting, and will be conducted in an indirect way.

Now then... in the "stress" interview...

WHAT IS THE "STRESS INTERVIEW"?

Although used infrequently, the stress interview is designed to bring out your responses to stress conditions or questions to which most people are unaccustomed. It is usually used during the later stages of the search process for higher-echelon jobs. The objective is not to make you feel uncomfortable, but to approximate the conditions under which you would work. It may be hard to take, but a stress interview is actually an excellent sign for your candidacy.

If you sense a stress interview is in the offing, it is imperative to recognize the importance of keeping your emotions under complete control. Relax and play the game.

So.... how'd I do?

HOW DO YOU HANDLE
"OFF THE WALL"
INTERVIEW QUESTIONS?

Be natural and keep cool. Give direct, honest answers. Either the interviewers are strange people (in which case you probably don't want the job), or they're trying to see if you get flustered or are easily unnerved.

Don't be afraid to be firm if the situation warrants it. Be your own man or woman--an oversubmissive attitude will win you no points. A polite, professional response (such as, "I don't think I see how that relates to my ability to perform") may help you move on to the next topic smoothly.

If asked a question that violates your civil rights, simply inform the interviewer calmly that he or she has crossed legal bounds. You may refuse to answer the question. Avoid confrontation during the interview (after all, there's little to be gained by making a scene). Seek legal advice after the interview to determine any further action you may wish to take.

WHO PAYS TRAVEL EXPENSES FOR OUT-OF-TOWN INTERVIEWS?

It depends. If the market for your field is tight, the employer will probably pay. If the market is glutted, chances are you'll pay your travel to and from interviews.

If the interviewer does not volunteer the information that the employer will reimburse travel costs, the candidate can generally assume that he or she must bear these expenses. A discreet confirmation of this is easy enough during a phone interview.

HOW DO YOU HANDLE
THE GROUP INTERVIEW?

The same way you handle the individual interview. Be natural; be yourself; be professional.

Group interviews sometimes take place at restaurants over lunch or dinner. Often the interviewers will be looking not only for answers to questions, but also how you handle yourself in a social situation. Here your social graces will play an important role. Of course, you should avoid consuming alcohol at such a meeting.

I suppose I could adjust my
salary demands a bit..

WHAT SALARY SHOULD YOU ASK FOR?

Let the interviewer bring up the subject. Know the salary range for the job under discussion. Avoid making salary demands before you are offered a position. You will probably be asked your present salary if you're working; if the new job does not entail additional responsibilities or skills, your current earnings may serve as the starting point for the employer.

You may wish to ask for a salary within a certain range, rather than for a specific figure. This may enable you to bracket your estimate of what the employer wishes to pay. Remember that, in the final analysis, salary is only one of many factors that will affect your job satisfaction.

As a matter of fact, we have a very good dental health plan for our employees...

WHEN SHOULD YOU DISCUSS FRINGE BENEFITS?

The same guidelines used in discussing salary questions are useful here.

Be sure you know what all the fringe benefits are before you accept the position. Fringe benefits can run up to thirty percent of starting salaries. Insurance and retirement plans, stock options, profit sharing, hospitalization, vacation, sick leave, sabbaticals, holidays, extra overtime compensation, retirement leaves, housing and transportation compensation, special loan benefits, and other items may be included in your package.

CHAPTER FOUR: MAKING YOUR DECISION

Around here we don't hold with the philosophy that your first job is not necessarily a lifetime job.

IS YOUR FIRST JOB YOUR LIFETIME JOB?

It's estimated that about one third of all hirees leave their first job within the first five years.

Some employers, of course, have higher turnover rates than others. You should appraise your job situation each year for the first five years, and every two to three years thereafter.

Here are some "yardsticks" you may wish to use in evaluating your situation:

> Professional development
> Work environment
> Associates
> Salary/Benefits
> Community
> Family
> Prestige
> Employer status

If the above are not meeting your expectations, it's probably time to contemplate a change.

AVOID POINTLESS JOB CHANGES

Job changes are inconvenient and usually costly; they should not be undertaken lightly. The term "out of the frying pan and into the fire" could have been coined expressly for those who make unnecessary job changes.

Foresight and advance work before you make the change can save you a lot of grief. Job changes virtually always work out best when they are properly planned.

What added financial benefits or visibility will you attain in the new position? Are the prospects for promotion better? Do you prefer the new work environment over your current one? Are the people the kind you'd like to work with? If the answers to these and similar questions don't present a clear advantage, rethink your strategy.

I suppose you're definite
about taking our offer...

WHAT IF YOU GET AN OFFER, ACCEPT IT, AND THEN RECEIVE A BETTER OFFER?

The easiest answer is, don't get yourself into this position in the first place. Avoid accepting an offer until you have finalized your decisions or negotiations on other offers.

Candidates often get themselves into terrible binds by mishandling the offer and acceptance phases. Going back on your word and "bailing out" of a job offer is one of the worst ways to start a career. Remember, many industries are surprisingly small. You're likely to run into people again. Do you want them to remember you as "the one who welched on us"?

By the same token, employers are expected to honor their offers if you accept. The employer can withdraw the offer prior to acceptance, however, with proper notice.

..AND..ARE..YOU..WILLING...TO...
MOVE...TO...ANY...GOD-FORSAKEN...

WILL YOU HAVE TO TAKE TESTS?

This is entirely dependent on the employer. Policies range from no tests to a full day of testing. Occasionally, employers will even ask you to take tests after they hire you.

Tests that are properly administered and interpreted can be of value both to the employer and the candidate. Unfortunately, some employers have not yet learned how to administer a testing program properly. This is a disadvantage that many job candidates will simply have to live with--though, to some degree, tests have fallen out of favor in recent years because of charges that some discriminate against minority groups.

While your employer can ask you to take a test to measure your skills and aptitudes, he or she cannot ask you questions during the interview about your marital status, heritage, or age (other than to confirm that you are over 18 years old).

Then I thought... Hey! Instead of me going to all your companies, why don't we all get together for a friendly talk?..

WHEN THE JOB SEEKS YOU OUT . . .

. . . give yourself a pat on the back.

This is an enviable position to be in. However, you should remember that candidates often fail to look over the entire range of possibilities, and sell themselves short in selecting the first offer that "falls into their laps."

If one employer seeks you out, chances are there are others who would be interested in you. Always look over the entire field before making a commitment. The field includes your current employer, if you have one. Some employers have to be nudged a little bit before giving salary increases or promotions. (Just be sure you have another job in hand before you nudge too hard!)

If you foul up, you're fired!
That takes care of your training
program – now get to work!

WHICH IS BETTER: JOINING A COMPANY WITH A FORMAL TRAINING PROGRAM, OR ONE WITHOUT SUCH A PROGRAM?

This can vary from company to company. Training programs are frequently helpful for the recent graduate or new entrant to the job market, and can help span the gap between college and industry.

While most of the larger corporations have well-designed programs, some on-the-job training can be a waste of time. A few discreet questions toward the end of an interview can give you a good idea about the company's policies. It will be a rare situation in which this factor alone tips the balance for any given candidate's choice.

WHAT IS THE USUAL PROCEDURE
WHEN AN OFFER IS MADE?

Initially, of course, you'll be interviewed by a host of people (typically including those from the personnel department); after that, you may be invited to a "plant visit," where you'll have the chance to meet higher-ups and perhaps take a few tests. You'll usually get the chance to see the area where you'd be working, as well.

It's somewhere near this stage of the cycle that the employer will usually let you know if the company is interested in you. This will be followed by a letter or phone call offering you a job. (Of course, if the employer is not interested, you'll receive a rejection letter.)

The offer will usually specify:

> Your title
> Your salary
> Starting date
> Location
> Date the offer expires
> Travel expense arrangement, if any
> Requested action on your part
> Breakdown of benefits
> Health examination requirements

Maybe you'd like to meet the boss a little later...

WHAT IS THE USUAL PROCEDURE
WHEN ACCEPTING A JOB?

It is best to complete all your interviews with employers you are interested in before accepting any offer. Research all your offers carefully so that you make the right acceptance.

Once your decision has been made, phone or write the employer telling him of your acceptance. A letter from the employer stating the conditions of the offer is customary. If you do not receive such a letter, it is a good idea to request one so that all parties will understand the details of the agreement. Such items as salary, benefits, starting date, physical exam arrangement, travel expenses, name of department and supervisor, and any other conditions of employment should be covered. Immediately contact all other potential employers explaining that you have accepted another offer.

If unforeseen circumstances develop (such as a second, more attractive job offer), call the first employer and explain your situation. If you make a reasonable request, it will usually be honored. (Do not invent fictitious "offers" in an attempt to boost your rate of pay. Such unethical behavior will usually come back to haunt you.)

CHAPTER FIVE: EVALUATING YOUR PROGRESS

Mobility is the key to success in business. Start moving.

HOW DO YOU EVALUATE YOUR PROGRESS?

Check the outside market periodically to determine your marketability.

If you haven't changed jobs or responsibilities in two or three years, you are probably ready to start thinking about your progress.

Remember, financial "progress" does not always lead to a better life. Define what you want out of life and equate your success against that standard, not someone else's idea of what it means to "make it."

Check salary data compiled by professional associations or your alumni placement office. You can usually get a good comparison of salaries from that source.

Look internally before going outside.

Isolate the problem. Abraham Maslow outlined five basic needs relevant to employment: physiological, social, self-actualization, personal esteem, and security. If you can't figure out why you are dissatisfied, Maslow's list might help you sort things out.

Any chance you could jog
by the office occasionally?

YOU DON'T FIND TIME--YOU MAKE IT!

As you develop in your job, the demands upon your personal time tend to increase--and the value of your time to do what you want to do becomes more important to you. This is compounded by the generally hectic pace of current society.

The smart employee will try to develop a career that allows room for such important areas of development as education, self-improvement, sports and/or exercise, and yes, even leisure time.

Seek work environments where it's possible for you to live the kind of life you want, not just make the kind of money you want.

All of this need not be accomplished at the expense of the employer; rather, these issues must be resolved to the mutual satisfaction of both you and management.

I understand you change jobs pretty regularly...

IS MOBILITY AN ADVANTAGE
IN GETTING AHEAD?

Planned mobility (i.e., moving on to a new job) is one of the best ways to get ahead in business, especially big business. Even lateral moves are usually better than no move at all. Early mobility and a fast start are usually necessary to get to the very top. Planned mobility, especially when marked by significant promotions, builds a positive reputation.

Most jobs can be mastered in two years; any time over that spent in the same job should be carefully appraised. Note, too, that staying at a company for less than a year raises questions about your commitment; several such experiences can detract from your resume. It is true, however, that the mere fact of having changed jobs and/or companies a number of times doesn't carry the stigma it once did.

You cut your chances for success if you do not take advantage of all opportunities as they develop. Mobility is usually best within one organization, but this is not always possible. The important point to remember is to change jobs for the right reason: career and personal growth.

Take a memo to the accounting department upstairs about the issue of executive visibility..

IS VISIBILITY BY TOP MANAGEMENT
AN ADVANTAGE IN GETTING AHEAD?

Executive visibility (being seen by top management) and mobility go hand in hand. If you've got what it takes and you combine your abilities with a certain healthy sense of self-promotion, your chances of success are increased. Rarely does a person get to the top without top management visibility. Remember, some jobs have great visibility, others very little. Plan so that the jobs you accept are ones that will allow you to get noticed.

You realize, I trust...that your major in Oriental Philosophy doesn't tie in a lot with business machines...

PREPARE YOURSELF FOR
MAXIMUM FLEXIBILITY

Job obsolescence is not imagined--it is real. It is becoming more evident with each passing year. To avoid obsolescence, personal growth and development is absolutely essential. Once you've gotten as broad a basic education as possible, continue to keep up-to-date by participating in seminars, continuing education courses, and reading trade journals. In short, plan to continue your education for the rest of your life.

INDEX

About the Authors

John D. Shingleton served as Placement Director at Michigan State University for 25 years, advising thousands of students and alumni on their careers. He has worked for several major employers and currently is consultant to numerous univerisities and employers primarily on the subject of employment. He has had the prestigious Applied Research Award named in his honor by the Midwest College Placement Association. The College Placement Council has also awarded him their first "Outstanding Professional" award. He has also written a career column for the Detroit Free Press for over four years. *WHICH NICHE?* is his sixth book.

Phil Frank is a freelance artist and syndicated cartoonist whose work is seen in more than 100 college newspapers and numerous daily newspapers and national magazines.

Martin Yate's new ground-breaking resume book.

Real resumes that produced real jobs...

Resumes that Knock 'em Dead

Martin John Yate

Every single resume in *Resumes that Knock 'em Dead* was used by a real individual within the last 18 months to successfully obtain a job.

Many of the resumes shown were successfully used to change careers; others resulted in dramatically higher salaries. Some produced both. For example, a man working as a $6-an-hour welder used his resume to obtain a $70,000-a-year sales position.

To serve as broad an audience as possible, Yate carefully chose resumes for the most commonly-sought positions on all levels.

Yate also reviews the marks of a great resume: what type of resumes is right for each applicant, what always goes in, what always stays out and why.

No other book provides the hard facts for producing an exemplary resume. No other book can produce resumes that knock 'em dead.

> I like this book! Job-hunters will like this book too! It offers specific, straightforward, easy-to-find answers to the detailed, nitpicky questions some resume-writers always have. And, with a collection of 150 actual resumes . . . what else could you ask for? A great companion to the author's interview guide.
>
> John Noble
> **Associate Director of Career Services**
> *Harvard University*

■ Paper, 8 1/2 X 11, 216 Pages, $7.95
■ ISBN: 1-55850-954-2

ORDER TOLL-FREE
1-800-USA-JOBS
IN MA: (617) 767-8100